The Little
Monet

Catherine de Duve

Discover the wonderful garden of Giverny

KATE'ART
EDITIONS

I am in ecstasy. Giverny is a splendid place for me!

CLAUDE MONET

In his studio at Giverny, Monet painted huge pictures that became some of the most famous paintings ever made. His inspiration came from the magnificent garden he had planted and his pond full of water lilies. Now as he wandered in the garden and sat by the pond, Monet thought back to the many good times he'd had with his family in the big pink house at Giverny.

He could still hear the children's laughter as they played hide and seek in the garden, and he remembered the fun they all had fishing in the river nearby.

Germaine, Suzanne, Blanche

Monet's home at Giverny was full of colour and activity. Marguerite, the cook, made delicious meals in the big blue and white kitchen. The family sat down to eat together in the bright yellow dining room. All the colours of the rainbow could be found outside in the garden. Monet loved living in the country.

Which part of Monet's house and garden do you like the best?

Kitchen

Dining Room

Garden

Bridge

Garden Entrance

Lily Pond

NORMANDY

Oscar-Claude Monet was born on the 14th of November in 1840. When he was five, his family moved to the seaside city of Le Havre in Normandy. At school, when he got bored, Monet drew funny pictures of his teachers. Soon he was selling caricatures of townspeople in a local shop. One day, Monet met the landscape painter *Eugène Boudin*, who became his mentor.

caricature

My studio?
This is my studio!

Monet and Boudin *were among the first artists to paint outdoors, instead of sketching scenes outside and later painting them in the studio. Paint tubes had recently been invented, making it easier for artists to paint anywhere they wanted.*

In France in the 1800s, women wore long dresses to the beach and carried parasols to shade themselves from the sun!

> *If I have indeed become an artist, I owe it to Eugène Boudin.*

Eugène Boudin

It is summer by the sea. Holidaymakers lounge in the sun and watch the boats go by. Some of the vessels on the horizon are sailing ships with tall masts. Others are more modern steamships, a recent invention! Can you tell which is which?

How many small boats are sailing nearby?
How many steamships do you see on the horizon?

PARIS!

At 18, Monet went to Paris to study art. Soon after, he was drafted and sent to Algeria to serve in the French army. He was fascinated by the intense light and dramatic colours of North Africa, but he soon became ill and was shipped home. On his return to Paris, he joined the art studio of Charles Gleyre, a famous Swiss artist. There he met Auguste Renoir and other young painters who shared his passion for art.

 Monet, Renoir and their friends soon began creating a new art style that became known as Impressionism.

Monet looked out the window of a friend's studio to paint this winter scene in Paris. He captured the hustle and bustle of the city with small, quick brush strokes. He made everything look a little out of focus, conveying a sense of movement. Horse-drawn carriages go by as people bundled in warm coats stroll along the boulevard. The whole scene pulses with energy!

Everything in the painting is just barely suggested. Look carefully! Can you find:

- ○ *a newspaper kiosk*
- ○ *a man selling balloons*
- ○ *drivers atop their carriages*
- ○ *a line of parked carriages*
- ○ *a top hat*
- ○ *trees along the boulevard*

A PICNIC IN THE WOODS

Times were hard for Monet. He wasn't selling any paintings and his parents were worried that he wouldn't be able to make a living as an artist. Monet wanted to prove himself by painting a huge work of art. He found inspiration in the nearby forest of Fontainebleau where he decided to paint a picnic scene. He asked his artist friends, Gustave Courbet and Frédéric Bazille, to pose for him. His two friends posed several times as different people!

How many men do you see in the scene?
Look closely at the tree bark.
Can you guess what kind of tree it is?

In 1866, Monet worked tirelessly to finish a painting for the big, annual art exhibition in Paris. His efforts paid off. The famous writer, Émile Zola, wrote a glowing review of his art and the two men became good friends.

Monet exhibited a painting of his future wife, Camille, in an elegant green dress.

What are the picnickers doing? How are they dressed? How would you like to go on a picnic in the woods in a long, fancy dress or in a suit?

In Monet's day, fashionable women wore long dresses made of luxurious fabrics. Create your own design for Camille's dress.

SUMMER FUN

onet and his family were poor! Auguste Renoir would sometimes bring them a loaf of bread, then the two friends would go out to paint. One Sunday, they set up their easels side by side along the river Seine. They painted the same scene at a favourite summer spot called *la Grenouillère*, which means "the frog pond." Young Parisians gathered there to dance, sing, and go for a swim.

Even though the waters of the Seine were already quite polluted, young people would jump in for a swim on hot summer days. They could also rent rowboats and set off from the round, floating dock. They called the dock *"le camembert"* because it reminded them of the round French cheese.

How is Monet's painting different from Renoir's? Who painted two ladies in long swimming outfits? a sailboat? two dogs? a man in a top hat?

RENOIR

SNOW

During the winter's of 1869, Monet returned to his family home in Normandy. It was very cold, but that did not stop him from going out with his easel, canvas, brushes, and paints to capture winter scenes. He painted the beaches, cliffs, fishing boats, storms at sea, and the countryside covered with snow.

Make up a story that takes place on a magical winter's day.

A little black and white bird sits on a gate, keeping Monet company as he paints. Shadows dance on the soft blanket of snow. A farmhouse is partially hidden by the trees powdered in white. Everything is still. Can you see footprints in the snow? Perhaps they are Monet's.

Snow may be white, but Monet painted its shadows and reflections in many colours. Can you find them all?

13

FLOATING STUDIO

London in the smog

In 1870, Claude and Camille were married. Then war broke out between France and Prussia. The young couple escaped to London with their little boy, Jean. Monet painted scenes of the Thames River bathed in smog. After the war, Monet and his family returned to France and settled in Argenteuil, a small town on the River Seine just outside Paris. Monet got a little boat and made it into a studio so he could float on the river and paint!

Claude Monet

From his boat, Monet painted *sailboat* races. He captured the boats' reflections in the river, along with the clear blue sky and the colourful houses along the riverbank. Is a sailboat race about to begin?

An official sailboat race is called a regatta.

Here are Monet's reflections. Draw and colour sailboats to go with each reflection.

LUNCH IN THE GARDEN

After a delicious lunch in the garden, the women stroll among the flowers while little Jean sits in the shade and plays with his blocks. How old is he? Is it almost time for his nap? The table has not yet been cleared. It makes a lovely *still life* for Monet to paint. Someone has found an unusual place to hang her hat.

Can you find the hat, the rose?

Wherever he settled, Monet grew flowers, and from these flowers paintings were born. The garden provided him with another set of colours, other textures and other dimensions.

Find where each piece of the puzzle fits in the painting.

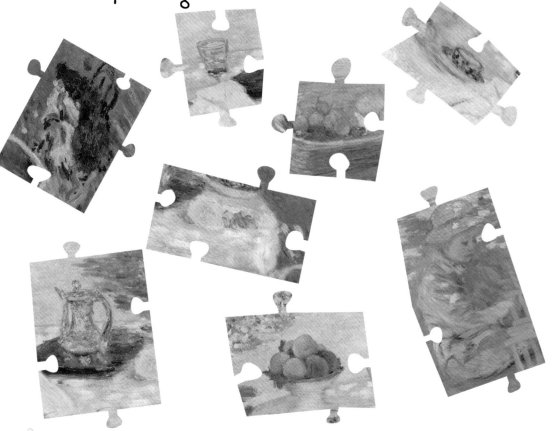

*A **still life** is a painting of things arranged on a table or chair. The artist captures the forms, colours, and light reflected on each object. Here Monet painted a freshly picked rose, a bowl of fruit, cups, napkins, a coffee pot… all bathed in dappled sunlight.*

FLOWERS

"It's a beautiful day," said Monet to his family. "Let's go for a walk!" He painted Camille and Jean coming down a hill through a field of poppies near their home. Jean is about six years old. Camille has her blue parasol. Would you like to be in this summer scene, playing in the field of flowers?

Discover the flowers from Monet's garden.
Which ones have you seen in a garden or
growing as wildflowers?

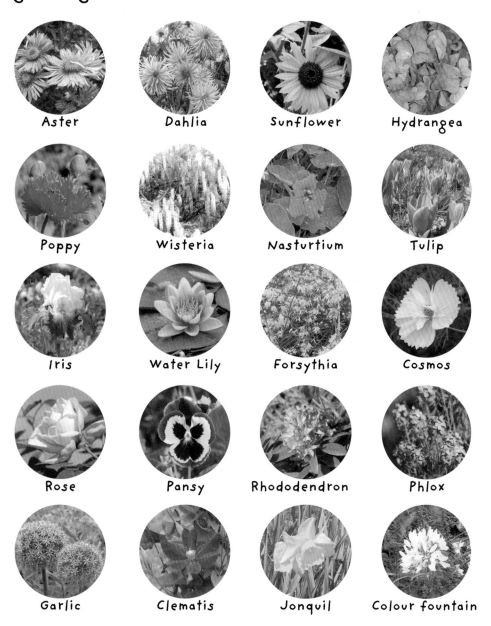

Aster	Dahlia	Sunflower	Hydrangea
Poppy	Wisteria	Nasturtium	Tulip
Iris	Water Lily	Forsythia	Cosmos
Rose	Pansy	Rhododendron	Phlox
Garlic	Clematis	Jonquil	Colour fountain

IMPRESSIONISM

This is the painting that gave the Impressionists their name!

Many young artists were not allowed to exhibit in the Salon, the official art exhibition held in Paris each year. So in 1874, Monet and his friends decided to organize their own exhibition where they could show the public their daring new style of painting, with its bright colours and bold brushstrokes. But the public was used to a traditional style of art in which everything was painted in sharp detail and with muted colours. They thought this new style looked sloppy and unfinished. One of the paintings Monet exhibited was called *Impression, Sunrise*.

An art critic, Louis Leroy, visited the new exhibition. He stopped in front of Monet's painting and exclaimed, "This isn't a painting! It's just a sketch, an impression!" In a nasty review, he wrote, "Wallpaper in its embryonic state is more finished than that seascape." He called the artists "impressionists." The critic meant it as an insult but Monet liked the name.

Painting impressions was what Monet most wanted to do. He worked hard to capture on his canvas the reflections of light that he saw in a particular moment. He said, "I am, and always will be, an Impressionist!"

Pissarro

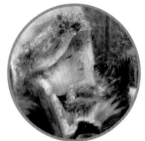
Renoir

Monet

Morisot

Degas

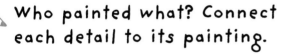
Who painted what? Connect each detail to its painting.

PAINTING IN SERIES

Monet liked to paint scenes of city life as well as country scenes. In the city, he painted the trains at St. Lazare station, billowing with steam. And he painted different versions of the cathedral in Rouen. Monet liked to choose one subject and paint many versions at different times of day. As the light changed from moment to moment, the colours Monet saw would change. He had to paint fast to capture the moment!

What time is it?

Morning

Evening

Monet paid a farmer to leave haystacks standing in his field for months so Monet could paint them in different seasons and in different light conditions. He often worked on five or six canvases at a time, switching from one to another as the sun climbed higher in the sky or ducked behind the clouds.

Monet painted 20 haystack pictures.
Colour these in different seasons.

In the snow

In the rain

In the sun

In springtime

23

PHOTO ALBUM

When Monet was a struggling young artist, he was invited to the chateau of a wealthy art collector, Ernest Hoschedé, to paint for him. A year later, Hoschedé went bankrupt and lost his chateau. His wife, Alice, and their five children had nowhere to live. Monet invited the Hoschedés to come live with him and his family.

In 1879, Monet's wife, Camille, died after a long illness. Monet later married Alice after her husband, Ernest, died. Between them, they had eight children.

Meet Claude and Alice and their families.

THE MONET FAMILY

Camille Doncieux (1847-1879) & Claude Monet (1840-1926)

Jean
(1867-1914)

Michel
(1878-1966)

THE HOSCHEDÉ FAMILY

Alice Raingo (1844-1911) & Ernest Hoschedé (1838-1891)

Marthe
(1864-1925)

Blanche
(1865-1947)

Suzanne
(1868-1899)

Jacques
(1869-1941)

Germaine
(1873-1968)

Jean-Pierre
(1877-1961)

Monet with a Japanese friend in a kimono.

In 1883, Monet rented the big, beautiful house in Giverny. He hung his collection of *Japanese prints* on the wall of the reading room. He was reminded of an art exhibit he had seen in Paris many years before.

*To make a **Japanese print**, the artist first carves an image in a woodblock then applies coloured inks to it and prints the image on paper. The artist can make many prints of the same picture. The bright colours and simple lines in Japanese prints inspired the Impressionists.*

How many fans are in the painting? Which one is not in the painting? Colour the blank fan.

In 1867, for the first time in Paris, there was a large exhibition of Japanese art, with folding screens, fans, and prints. Monet was entranced by what he saw. Years later, he painted his wife, Camille, in a red kimono holding a Japanese fan.

THE GARDEN

Monet finally became a famous artist! He sold enough paintings to buy the house in Giverny. He painted the shutters and doors bright green and created a big, lush garden. It was a lot of hard work. Claude Monet had a huge garden to plant and tend! Monet gardened the way he painted. He planted groups of flowers to create harmonies of colour.

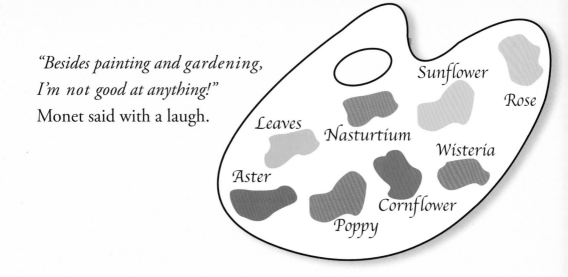

"Besides painting and gardening,
I'm not good at anything!"
Monet said with a laugh.

Match the colours on the palette
with the flowers in the garden.

WATER LILIES

Monet created a "water garden" near his house. He had a huge hole dug and diverted water from a nearby river to make a pond. He grew water lilies in the pond and planted weeping willows beside it. And he had a Japanese bridge built across the pond. Monet loved to watch the reflections of the water lilies and trees in the water. To friends he would say, "Come see my masterpiece!"

Monet said, "Try to forget what object you have before you: a tree, a house, a field. Merely think, here is a little square of blue, here is an oblong of pink, here a streak of yellow... and paint what you see."

Find the different brushstrokes. What did Monet paint, using up and down strokes? Sideways strokes? Little dabs of colour?

Claude Monet painted until the very end of his life. He died at Giverny in 1926, at 86 years old. By then, he had become one of the most important and beloved artists of the 20th century.

Text: Catherine de Duve
Translated by: Wenda O'Reilly, Ph.D.
Graphic design: Kate'Art Editions
Concept and production: Kate'Art Editions
Proofreading: Nathalie Trouveroy

PARIS: Musée d'Orsay: *In the "Norvégienne",* 1887: p. 2 - *Luncheon on the Grass,* 1865: p. 9 - *The Magpie,* 1869: pp. 12-13 - *Régatta at Argenteuil,* 1872: p. 15 - *The Luncheon,* 1873: pp. 16-17 - *Poppies at Argenteuil,* 1873: p. 18 - *Rouen Cathedral, Portal and the Tour d'Albane, full sun, harmony in blue and gold,* 1894: p. 22 *Haystacks, end of summer, morning effect,* 1891: p. 23 - *Monet's Garden, Irises,* 1900: p. 28 - *Water-Lilies, harmony in green,* 1899: p. 30 - **Musée Marmottan:** *Water-Lilies, Evening effect,* 1897-1898: cover (detail), p. 1, pp. 30 -31, *The writer Jules François Félix Husson, a.k.a. Champfleury, after Nadar,* env.1858: p. 4 - *Jules de Prémaray (editor-in-chief of "La Patrie") after Nadar,* env. 1858: p. 4 - *Impression, rising sun,* 1872-1873: p. 20 *Water-Lilies,* 1916-1919: p.30

LONDON: The National Gallery: *On the Beach at Trouville,* 1870: p. 4 - **ZURICH: Kunsthaus Zürich:** *Houses of Parliament, Sunset,* 1904: p. 14 - **MOSCOW: Pushkin Museum:** *Luncheon on the Grass,* 1865: p. 8 **BREMEN: Kunsthalle:** *Camille or Woman in the Green Dress,* 1866: p. 9 - **OTTERLO: Kröller-Müller Museum:** *The Studio-Boat,* 1874: p. 14 - **NEW YORK: Metropolitan Museum of Art:** *The Terrace at Sainte-Adresse,* 1867: p. 5 - *La Grenouillère,* 1869: p.10 - *The Water-Lily Pond,* 1899: p. 31 - **KANSAS CITY: The Nelson Atkins Museum of Art:** *The Boulevard des Capucines,* 1873: pp. 6-7 - **CHICAGO: The Art Institute of Chicago:** *The Artist's Home at Argenteuil,* 1873: p. 17 - *Gare Saint-Lazare, the Normandy Train,* 1877: p. 22 *Haystacks at the end of summer, evening effect,*1891: p. 23 - **BOSTON: Museum of Fine Arts:** *Rouen Cathedral, Portal and the Tour d'Albane,* 1894: p. 22 - *La Japonaise (Camille Monet in a Japanese Costume),* 1875: pp. 26-27 - **WASHINGTON, D.C.: National Gallery of Art:** *Monet's Garden in Vétheuil,* 1881: p. 21 - *The Japanese Bridge,* 1899: p.30 - **TOKYO: The National Museum of Western of Art:** *Water-Lilies,* 1914: cover

Private Collection: *Camille Monet and a child in the garden at Argenteuil,* 1875: p. 17 - *Claude Monet's Self-Portrait,* 1886: p. 25 - **Photographs:** *Claude Monet in his studio with the "Waterlilies" at Giverny,* vers 1921: p. 2, p. 25 © Archives Durand-Ruel, Paris - **Musée Marmottan:** *Claude and Alice in Venice, October 1908:* p. 25 - *Claude Monet , 1913:* cover, p. 25 - **International Museum of Photography, New York:** p. 25 **Archives Walther, Alling:** *A Walk in Giverny with Mrs. Huroki:* p. 25, 26 - **RMN:** p. 31 © Fondation Claude Monet: pp. 2, 3 © Photo Kate'Art Editions: cover, p. 3, 19, 29.

Other painters:
CHICAGO: The Art Institute of Chicago: Eugène Boudin, *Approaching Storm,* 1864: p. 5 - **LONDON: Courtault Institute Galleries:** Edgar Degas, *Two dancers on a stage,* 1874: p. 21 - **PARIS: Musée d'Orsay:** Berthe Morisot: *The Cradle,* 1872: p. 21 - **OXFORD: Ashmolean Museum:** Camille Pissarro: *View from my window, Éragny,* 1888: p. 21 - **STOCKHOLM, National Museum:** Auguste Renoir, *La Grenouillère,* 1869: p. 11 - **WASHINGTON, D.C.: Collection Phillips:** Auguste Renoir, *Luncheon of a Boating Party,* 1880-1881: p. 21

We wish to thank : Mrs. Gerald Van Der Kemp, Claudette Lindsey, Laurent Echaubard and the Fondation Claude Monet at Giverny, Eric Vaes, Claire Toulgouat, Priscilla d'Oultremont, Wenda O'Reilly, Ph. D., Julie Stouffs and all those who assisted in making this book.